HURT

EQUIPPING CHILDREN FOR LOSS

D1636936

THERA STORM, LCSW

ILLUSTRATIONS BY ASHLEY & ALEX SCHARR

Hurt: Equipping Children for Loss.

ISBN: 978-1-09831-364-7

Printed in the U.S.A.

Address all inquiries to Thera Storm, LCSW

(858) 829-0060

tstorm@claritycorp.us

www.claritycorp.us

Dear Adult,

The question is not "if" your children will experience loss in their lifetime. It's "when."

I don't say this to be morbid. We all experience loss because we are human! Life is filled with many transitions, disappointments, and grief. Loss includes misplacing our favorite toy, moving, divorce, death, and everything in between.

Do you struggle with talking to children about grief? You're not alone. Many of us (including teachers, therapists, and parents) find that talking about loss is challenging and uncomfortable.

It doesn't have to be! In fact, we have many opportunities to address grieving children in a compassionate way. A child who is heard and validated grows up to be a compassionate, emotionally grounded adult.

In this book, we learn how easy it is to equip our children to express their emotions and provide comfort to others rather than use bandages to cover up the pain.

From my heart to yours,

Thera Storm, LCSW

Dedicated to Carlisle Joy. You are my favorite little human. Thank you for showing me that being seen, heard, validated, and hugged is better than any of those fancy superhero bandages.

Love, Mommy

Hi. I'm Bert.

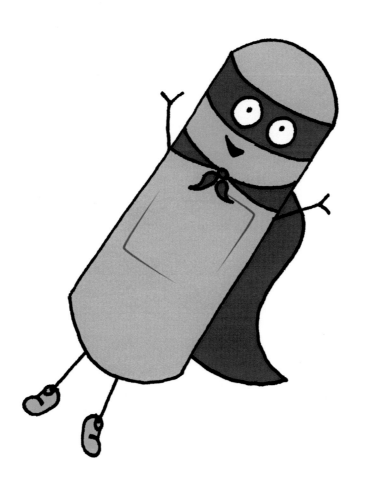

I'm pretty much a superhero.

I'm always on the lookout for anyone who is hurt.

That way, I can see when someone needs me.

(Sometimes I HEAR it, too!)

Scraped knee?

That's a job for me!

See? All better!

Mission
Accomplished!

Hmmm...

I do not see a booboo. Do you?

Did that help?

What hurts?

Did that help?

Oh, this little girl definitely looks hurt!

Did that help?

I have an idea!

He just needs some bandage FRIENDS!

Did that help?

All of these faces
show that something's
not right...

Yet, there isn't a single booboo in sight!

I FEEL SAD. LONELY. HEARTBROKEN. STUPID. UNCOOL. CONFUSED. SCARED. INVISIBLE. LEFT OUT.

I'm confused! I'm upset!
I'm starting to CRY!

My bandages aren't helping,
and I don't know why!!

Did that help?

Silly Bert!
Bandages cannot help when
it's THE HEART that is hurt!

A hug.

A kind smile.

A listening ear.

Being a friend.

Just being near.

It's HUMAN to become upset and sad.

No wonder sticking on a bandage
just made my friends mad!

So now when I sense that someone is hurt, instead of a bandage, I say, "Hi! I'm Bert!"

"I'm here to help!"
and for a good place
to start, I ask, "Is this
a booboo, or a pain
in your heart?"

Healing can be easy
but a lot depends
on sharing your feel-
ings and having
good friends.

Did that help?

As much as it hurts us to see children grieving, equipping them to deal with loss means that we have to lovingly embrace the pain WITH them.

Although a bad haircut or losing a stuffed animal may seem insignificant, those are actually grief-worthy events. These "small" experiences are where children learn how to deal with all losses. If they're taught to avoid the pain, hide the tears, hide from the hurt, and mask the sadness... then that's how they'll deal with grief their entire adult life.

As much as I'd like to jump over, around, or under grief, the healthiest way to navigate grief is go through it.

Thank you for taking the time to read this book. For more information on grief to include blogs, videos, resources, etc., please visit my website at claritycorp.us.

Co-illustrators Ashley and Alex Scharr live in
New Orleans with their cat, "Kitty." Both have varied
creative outlets from music and frame making to
drawing and watercolor.

Thera Storm is a licensed clinical social worker with a "grief lens." Thera believes that most issues that people carry around with them as adults are due to unresolved grief, which snowballs as we get older and encounter additional losses. Thera has been trained as an advanced grief recovery specialist from the Grief Recovery Institute. Thera provides the The Grief Recovery Method to clients all over the world through an online platform. Thera is a military spouse currently living in San Diego, CA, with her husband (active duty Marine) and their daughter, Carlisle, who brings lots of laughs, joy, entertainment, and inspiration.